Managing Money with Purpo$e

By: Junior C.A Pedro, FCCA

Author: Junior C.A Pedro FCCA

Email: juniorpedro@yahoo.com

TABLE OF CONTENTS

Preface

Thanks be to God for the knowledge and inspiration to write this book. It is an honour and privilege to be chosen by Him to provide information to those people who desire to become better financial stewards. Secondly, I extend heartfelt appreciation and thanks to my pastor Apostle Dr. Dexter James for granting me the opportunity to co-author the book, "Common Sense Approach to Increase", my initiation into writing. I also like to acknowledge Edson Eastmond who gave freely of his time and expertise to edit the text and provide valuable comments.

The idea for this book came from a presentation I did at a conference in St. Marteen in 2013. The conference's theme "Money Meets Purpose" gave me the inspiration to start writing. God created each one of us with a specific purpose. The word of God says in Jeremiah 1:5 "Before I formed thee in the belly I knew thee; and before thou camest forth out of the womb I sanctified thee, and I ordained thee a prophet unto the nations." (KJV)

I have experienced firsthand many of the issues, challenges, risk and opportunities businesses and individuals face daily as it pertains to many types of decisions including financial decisions. We all want to grow, improve and be successful but many of us struggle with managing our cash efficiently. Most individuals never take the time to prepare or understand the essential need and importance of a budget in our daily lives.

Your money is your responsibility, but do you understand the purpose of your money? Time and experience has taught me, where there is no clear direction money chooses its own path without consulting its owner. However; when one establishes a clearly defined purpose for money it brings to its owner increased wealth. As such it's important that each person understand the purpose of their money as it places them in the best position to manage it successfully.

I am a firm believer in the phrase, "if you are not relevant then you are serving no useful purpose." As such, this book is a practical guide for individuals and entrepreneurs interested in matching their budget with purpose. A budget needs to match purpose to be useful to the individual and the business owner.

I encourage you to take up the challenges presented throughout the book with an open mind.

Glossary of Terms

Asset- Any possession that has value in an exchange.

Attainable- When you identify goals that are most important to you, you begin to figure out ways you can make them come true. You develop the correct desire, attitudes, abilities, skills, and financial capacity to reach them.

Budget- An estimation of the income and expenses over a specified future time.

Cost- The expenditure of funds or use of property to acquire or produce a product or service.

Data- Facts or information used usually to calculate, analyze, or plan something.

Debt- Is an obligation to repay borrowed money.

Deficit- Essentially refers to the difference between cash inflows and outflows.

Economic Policy- A government policy for maintaining economic growth and tax revenues.

Expenditure- An amount of money that is spent on something.

Expense- The cost incurred in or required for something.

Financial Position- The account status of a firm's or individual's assets, liabilities, and equity positions as reflected on its financial statement.

Fixed Expenses- A cost that does not change with an increase or decrease in the amount of goods or services produced. Fixed costs are expenses that have to be paid by a company, independent of any business activity.

Income- The money a person makes from labour, investment, or any other source, especially in the course of a year.

Invoice- An invoice or bill is a commercial document issued by a seller to a buyer, indicating the products, quantities, and the agreed prices for products or services the seller has provided the buyer.

Liabilities- A financial obligation or the cash outlay that must be made at a specific time to satisfy the contractual terms of such an obligation.

Measurable- The thought behind this is that if a goal is not measurable, it is not possible to know whether a team is making progress toward successful completion.

Net Worth- The value of the assets you own, including but not limited to cash, securities, personal property, real estate, and retirement accounts, subtracted from your liabilities, or what you owe in loans and other obligations.

Plan- A set of actions that have been thought of as a way to do or achieve something.

Relevant- A goal that supports or is in alignment with other goals would be considered as a relevant goal.

Resources- A supply of something (such as money) that someone has and can use when it is needed.

Revenue- Money that is made by or paid to a business or an organization.

Self-Assessment- An assessment or evaluation of oneself or one's actions, attitudes, or performance as it relates to a predetermined standard.

Self-Examination- The study of one's own behaviour and motivations.

Specific- This means the goal is clear and unambiguous; without vagaries and platitudes. To make goals specific, they must tell a team exactly what is expected, why is it important, who is involved, where is it going to happen and which attributes are important.

Steward- A person whose job is to manage the land and property of another person.

Surplus- A surplus often occurs in a budget, when expenses are less than the income.

Time-bound A commitment to a deadline, which helps a team, focus their efforts on the completion of the goal on or before the due date. A time-bound goal is intended to establish a sense of urgency.

Variable Expenses- A corporate expense that varies with production output. Variable costs are those costs that vary depending on a company's production volume; they rise as production increases and fall as production decreases.

Introduction

" I exhort therefore, that, first of all, supplications, prayers, intercessions, and giving of thanks, be made for all men; For kings, and for all that are in authority; that we may lead a quiet and peaceable life in all godliness and honesty. For this is good and acceptable in the sight of God our Saviour;" 1 Timothy 2:1-3 KJV

The Lord has instructed us through His word that we should pray for those in authority. Do you take time to pray for the government and leaders in your country? The government holds the position of financial steward assigned with the responsibility for preparing and presenting a budget each year. When you are praying for those in authority ask God to grant them wisdom to be good financial stewards.

In modern industrial economies, the budget is a key instrument for the execution of government economic policies. In effect, they decide how and where a country's limited resources will be allocated. The main purpose of the government's budget is to achieve when and where possible, a positive balance between revenue and expenditure in alignment with its economic policies. This however; due to many constraints and competing interests may not always be possible.

An increasing trend around the world today, in the Caribbean and even here, in Trinidad and Tobago is budget deficits. A budget deficit is a situation where the government expenditure exceeds income. In the United States of America, the budget deficit for 2012 totalled, $ 1.1 trillion , United States dollars, while in Trinidad and Tobago it amounted to $ 6,675.8 million Trinidad and Tobago dollars.

Can this state of affairs be a good for a country, the region and the world? Many argue that added spending is necessary for short-term survival, while others oppose it given that it will be to the detriment of future generations.

Whichever side of the equation you lean towards apply the aforementioned scenario to your personal life and business. Do you believe an individual or business should be spending more than they earn? If you agree, there is no need to read further.

A government's current and future performance is measured by the budget put forward annually. How do you measure the financial performance of yourself, family, business, or non-profit organization? Do you have a budget?

Whether you are the government responsible for managing the resources of a country, an entrepreneur, an employee, a husband and wife team, a young university student, a single parent, grandparents, or non-profit organization (no matter what your situation and position is in life) a budget should be prepared once annually and in some cases weekly, fortnightly, or even monthly. If you have not completed a budget before now, then I encourage you to start, but if you have, then I applaud you and encourage you to continue. Significant benefits lay ahead.

Before you get involved with this book, I need your written answers to the following questions.
1. Do you need a budget and if yes, why?
2. What is your purpose for doing a budget?
3. What do you want to gain from reading this book?

There is no shortage of information in printed form as well as available online on the subject of budgeting. So why are there individuals and businesses today who function without a budget? A budget is such an important tool in measuring both personal and business financial success, yet it is greatly under-utilized.

The aim of this book is to motivate individuals and business owners to place a higher priority on budgeting. My desire is that after reading this book that it would inspire and encourage more individuals and businesses to create budgets as required and to use them in fulfilling their purpose.

As you read the following chapters, I encourage you to complete the questions and not focus on getting to the end of the book. This guide will help you to be a better financial steward personally and in business helping you to match your budget with your purpose.

God has appointed us as stewards; as such, we are to be good financial stewards of what He has given us to mange. The parable of the talents in the Bible in Matthew 24:14-29 speaks directly to this matter where each servant is given talents according to his ability. It goes on further to state that each servant was responsible to give an account to the master for his stewarding of the given talents. The account goes on to show that there was one servant who was unproductive and had no plan and when he reported on his stewardship, the master took away the talent from him. I beg you do not be like the servant who did nothing with his talent.

The greatest value does not come from reading the book but putting the things learnt into practice.

A budget entails three simple steps, a self-assessment, a plan and preparing the budget.

Have you ever done a self-assessment?

Chapter 1: Self-Assessment

"Examine yourselves, whether ye be in the faith; prove your own selves. Know ye not your own selves, how that Jesus Christ is in you, except ye be reprobates?" 2 Corinthians 13:5 KJV

The bible verse above speaks about us examining ourselves. To gain an in-depth understanding of yourself and business the first step is self-examination. I am sure you are excited and anxious to start working on the budget. It will be careless of me to start at the end (completed budget) and not take time to first nurture you. When the first part is completed, we can work our way through to the end. Budgeting is a process, like every process you start at the beginning.

Before starting the budgeting exercise, each individual and business must have an understanding of his or her current financial position. To move from your present condition to the final destination (a completed budget), a starting point needs to be established. As such, our budgeting journey begins with a self-assessment exercise.

What is the purpose of a self-assessment? The aim of the self-assessment is for you to understand in detail your current financial position, both personally and as a business owner. Given their intimate knowledge, the individuals best suited to complete the self-assessment is the individual or business owner. It requires historical data and current information which the individual and business owner will have readily available.

To gain the greatest value from this exercise, you need to be honest, truthful, fair, accurate and detailed as possible. Failure to get the first part of the puzzle right, may never allow us to reach the final destination of a well-prepared budget and the reality of a budget fit for our individual purpose may not be achieved. I encourage you to take the time as you read to fully complete the self-assessment. This part of the process cannot be delegated or by-passed, you are the owner – you are the steward.

The self-assessment exercise involves completing a detailed listing of your assets, liabilities, income and expenses. The information gathered from this exercise will help you at the budgeting stage.

Do you know your net worth? Why having an understanding of your net worth important?

Chapter 2: Assessing your net worth

*"The rich ruleth over the poor, and the
borrower is servant to the lender."*
Proverbs 22:7 KJV

Start each day with this confession "I will not
be a servant to the borrower". The time has come
for you to live a debt free life. Make wise choices
today to free yourself, family and business of debt.
In business, net worth is the total assets minus total
liabilities of the individual or business. A good
starting place I recommend to clients is to begin
listing their assets. Assets consist of the things you
own for e.g. land, car, home, furniture, equipment,
money, etc... The assets listed need to be assigned
values to complete this exercise.

Those of us who hold on to bills, now is a good
time to take them out of the shoebox. These bills
will give us the purchase cost of the items. If you
unable to find the bills, no need to worry just
estimate the cost or value to replace the asset.

The table below is a guide to complete your
assets listing; additional lines can be added if
required.

Assets	Amount
Land	
Car	
Home	
Furniture	
Equipment	
Money	
TOTAL	

The next step is to identify your liabilities; these are the amounts owed to third parties, other persons or institutions. This includes loans, mortgages, outstanding credit cards payments, hire purchases, money owed to friends, family, etc...Many individuals borrow from friends and family and do not repay. Do not fall into this category; not only you would be a servant to the lender for life but your legacy will be one of which fingers can be pointed at you as being a defaulter of loans . An updated balance on these amounts need to be obtained and tabulated. It may mean requesting information from the bank, mortgage company and other lending agencies.

The table below is a guide to complete your liabilities listing, lines can be added if required.

Liabilities	Amount
Loans	
Mortgages	
Credit Cards	
Hire Purchase	
Monies borrowed from Family, Friends, etc.	
TOTAL	

When you complete your listing of the assets and liabilities in the respective tables inclusive of the amounts of each table, a total is then tabulated for each column. If the total amounts owed (liabilities) are greater than the value of things you own (assets), your net worth is negative. It therefore means the lenders and creditors are financing your livelihood and business. There is no need to panic, all is not lost, and we can fix this situation.

Why is this not a good position for yourself and business? If the lenders and creditors should demand their monies to be repaid today, then you and your business could be forced into liquidation. The resulting end is that years of hard work and toil are gone in vain with nothing to show. Is this your position right now? I am willing to work with you to change this position.

Are your expenses greater than income? Are you running a budget deficit like the government?

Chapter 3: Surplus or Deficit

*"Will a man rob God? Yet ye have robbed me.
But ye say, Wherein have we robbed thee? In
tithes and offerings. Ye are cursed with a curse:
for ye have robbed me, even this whole nation."
Malachi 3:8-9 KJV*

Do you pay tithes and offerings? If you do not
then you are robbing the creator, the one who gave
you life, resources and the ability to get and steward
wealth. When reviewing your expenses pay
extremely close attention to the amount that goes to
God. Do not bring a curse upon yourself and
business by not following this biblical principle.
The next stage of the self-assessment is to compute
your monthly income and expenditure. This
involves an in-depth review of bank statements,
payslips, invoices, past bills and even memory to
obtain a value that is accurate and includes all
income and expenses for the day, week, month or
year or period that you are considering.

Income is funds received whether daily,
weekly, fortnightly or monthly from your employer
or business. Income may include salary and wages,
commissions, bonuses, gratuity, overtime, pensions
etc...For individuals this may be the simplest part of
the process as most incomes are fixed each month.

The people that are self-employed and own or
partly own a business, this may be more

complicated. I recommend businesses owners and self-employed persons to review their income over the last six months and calculate the average to find their monthly income figure.

The table below is a guide to complete your income; lines can be added if required.

Income	Amount
Salary & Wages	
Commissions	
Bonuses	
Gratuity	
Overtime	
Pensions	
TOTAL	

Moving on to the final stage of the self-assessment, which entails listing your expenses. For many this may pose the most challenging because most of us do not keep financial records. Starting today keep a note pad and start recording on a daily basis each item of expenditure. You will be surprised at where your money is spent.

Expenses can be divided into two categories fixed and variable. Fixed expenses stay constant while variable expenses vary each month. Why are we separating fixed and variable expenses? The aim is to manage variable expenses as these can get out of control if not managed properly. For example many persons spend money on fast food from time to time, though the amounts may be small over time the cost does add up.

Take the time and list your fixed expenses for e.g. rent, mortgage, loan payments, car payments, insurance premiums. Secondly, the variable expenses which includes; electricity, telephone, groceries, fuel, entertainment etc...

The table below is a guide to complete your expenses, lines can be added if required.

Fixed Expenses	Amount
Rent/Mortgage	
Loan Payments	
Car Payments	
Insurance Premium	
TOTAL	
Variable Expenses	
Electricity	
Telephone	
Groceries	
Fuel	
Entertainment	
Fast Food	
TOTAL	

You have updated income and expenses table(s). How does your current position reflect when your income is compared against expenditure? Is there a surplus or a deficit? A surplus position is great news, however, if you are running a deficit budget like the government it needs to be addressed sooner rather than later.

The information gathered at this stage is very important to the budgeting process. The data and information here will be used as reference when preparing your budget.

What new things have you learnt from the self-assessment exercise about yourself, family and business?

Chapter 4: Self-Assessment Review

"What gets measured gets managed."
Peter Drucker – Management Consultant

Thus far, a lot of time has been spent reading and recording during the self-assessment stage. It may have been tedious at the start but it is time well spent helping you to understand the current financial position of yourself and or business. The information gained and the new found understanding of your financial position will be invaluable as you begin to chart a new direction for the benefit of yourself, to those for whom you are responsible to and responsible for.

Take the time to reflect on the following questions.
1. Are your liabilities greater than your assets?
2. What are your major liabilities?
3. Are your expenses greater than your income?
4. What are your major items of expenditure?
5. Are your expenses too high?

If your liabilities are greater than your assets, you need to work on reversing this position and to change the direction of the trajectory. The aim is to make sure your assets exceeds your liabilities. You did a great job at identifying your major liabilities, the next step is working to reduce and eliminate them, and the choice is yours. This will improve your personal and business net worth. The Bible says that a good man leaves an inheritance for his children's children (Proverbs 13:22). You have a responsibility to lay up for the next generation we are duty bound to make it better for our children. Our decisions in the past and the ones that we make now will determine the value of the inheritance that we lay up for our children.

Are your expenses greater than your income? Is this the current position of your personal finances and that of your business? May I remind you that a budget deficit means that you are utilizing future income? This position cannot be sustained over the medium to long-term period and as such, you must treat with this problem now. Take the time, make the effort to review your expenses, to find areas in which you can reduce spending or find ways to increase your income – remember Proverbs 13:22.

I trust the self-assessment exercise has provided you with new information and facts. Congratulations on completing the self-assessment, now you are qualified to move to the next stage planning. There is no need to get worried we are one-step closer to the budget stage.

Do you have an idea of your purpose in life, business, and family?

Chapter 5: The Plan

"For I know the thoughts that I think toward you, says the Lord, thoughts of peace and not of evil, to give you a future and a hope" Jeremiah 29:11. KJV

"Those who fail to plan, plan to fail"
Author Unknown

The earlier chapters laid the foundation in helping you to understand yourself and business. God has a plan for your life and business. Spend time in prayer daily asking him to reveal his plan for yourself, family and business and as He speaks, be 100% obedient. You need to start looking towards the future.

Do you have vision for your business, life and family? Hope I did not catch you off guard with this one. Where are you taking your family and business, if you are not sure, then where you are going? My grandmother always said to me "Son, if you do not know where you are going any road can take you there." This saying is so very true.

To move from the present position to that place in the future requires a plan. Many individuals and businesses today are operating without a plan. Do you have a plan for your life, family and business? So now, you are wondering why you are struggling to enjoy a comfortable life and to grow your business. The purpose of a plan is to provide you with the road map for life and business.

The starting point of any venture in your life and in business is a good plan. Strange enough most individuals and businesses never allocate the time or priority to planning whether it be in purchasing a car, buying a new home or even getting into business. This is the most important and yet the least amount of time is spent in formulating a plan.

A well thought out plan is your road map to becoming successful. It should show the strengths, weaknesses, risks, opportunities, and threats of the individual and business. The plan challenges you to look at the present and define the access to the future. Remember in our planning seek the mind of the Lord, a perfect example of this is King David, in everything that he did, he would enquire of the Lord, in how it should be done! Remember we are part of his legacy, and we should adhere to the examples left to us in the Word of God.

A plan though does not guarantee success. It enables you to save time, money and resources resulting from poor decisions. Are you or your business operating without a plan? This is a sure recipe for failure. Many have said, "I have been in business for many years without a plan and I have survived". This is great but how many times you said to yourself if I thought of this earlier, I could have made a better decision.

So my question to you, why are you so afraid to put your thoughts on paper? A written and documented plan is so essential if you are serious on being successful. How can you be serious on convincing others of your plan if you are unable to write it where other persons can understand it and follow?

Your plan is essentially the guide to take you to that place where you see yourself, family and business in the future. As the visionary / steward, others must be able to follow you without a measure of doubt but how can they follow without a written plan?

There is no reason for you to delay any longer, let us start writing your plan right now; no need to postpone it any longer. So get out your note pad, iPad, tablet, laptop, and let us start working together on your plan.

What is your financial plan?

Chapter 6: Financial Plan

"And the Lord answered me, and said, Write the vision, and make it plain upon tables, that he may run that readeth it." Habakkuk 2:2 KJV

How many people do you know personally that have good plans in their minds? The Bible speaks to writing the vision down and making it plain so that others can run with it. Take the time to write down the plan for your life, family and business.

While undertaking the self-assessment you may have realised areas that need improvement. The aim of the financial plan is to move you from the present to the place where you see yourself, family and business in the future. The three key elements for your financial plan are; purpose, goals and period.

What is the purpose of your financial plan? To stay focus, your financial plan must have a purpose. This purpose is closely connected to your business and personal vision. This makes each plan unique because no two individuals or businesses are the same. Start today by stating the purpose of the financial plan for your business and personal life.

The next key step is to set goals. What are your financial goals? For an individual it may be; decrease/eliminate debt, increase/improve assets value, reducing expenses and or increase income. The goal for a business may be to obtain financing, increase revenue, manage expenses, and or reduce debt. The goals of each individual and business owner are tailored to meet his or her specific requirements. What is the most important goal for yourself and business?

The final step is to set up periods to achieve the goals. Each goal must have a target completion date. It is important to include the time as it sets a timeframe within which the individual and business need to accomplish the goal. Without a timeline the goals is just a shopping list. When setting your financial goals they need to be SMART. This means each goal must be Specific, Measurable, Attainable, Relevant, and time bound (SMART). What is the final date to achieve your financial goal?

Your financial plan will take you from that place of lack into a place of prosperity abundance once managed well. It will take you out from debt to a debt free living. It will deliver you from that place of barely getting by to surplus. Take the time to plan and see your future become a reality each day you live.

A budget can be completed without a plan, however; the budget will lack focus, direction and purpose. Ensuring there is a documented plan is a critical element of the budgeting process. I urge you strongly to have a documented plan. A good plan forces you to look forward into the future at the opportunities and risks, knowing that you have considered where you want to go and what you want to achieve. The plan should include the vision of the ideal position of where you see yourself and business in the future.

We have spent valuable time dealing with your financial plan. Every morning when you wake up, make a declaration; "I am committed to seeing my financial plan become a reality". We need to commit this to the Lord, as said in Proverbs 3:6, "in all thy ways acknowledge him, and he will direct thy paths" and in 1 Peter 5:7, Casting all your care upon him; for he careth for you".

You have completed the financial plan and you are one step closer to the budget. I trust now that you appreciate the importance of a plan. Take the time to reflect on the following questions.
1. Where do you want to be in next five years?
2. Where do you want to live?
3. Do I need more education?
4. How much do you expect to save in next five years?
5. How much do you expect to earn in the next five years?
6. How much do I plan to give over the next five years?
I believe that the planning exercise has provided the road map to your financial goals. Consider yourself a successful candidate to start the budget phase.
Have you ever completed a budget? What is a budget?

Chapter 7 Budget

"For which of you, intending to build a tower, sitteth not down first, and counteth the cost, whether he have sufficient to finish it?" Luke 14:28 KJV

When you started your business, did you take the time to figure out the cost? Before you got married did you spend time figuring out the cost to maintain a family? Most people start businesses and projects without first taking the time to figure out the cost. The Bible says to us that before we begin, we should count the cost first. In essence, we should first do a budget.

I did my first personal budget back in 2004, on post-it notes. Since then it has grown with me and is a valuable tool in helping me to manage my personal finances. I needed to get a handle on my money having to manage renting, school and living expenses. In my career as an accountant and financial advisor, I have and continue to be involved in creating and reviewing budgets for companies.

Most times when we think budget, it is seen as something complicated. Hence the reason so many individuals and businesses fail to do a budget and shy away from it due to misinformation, lacking of understanding or fear of facing the results of a well-done and accurate self assessment. Do you have a challenge with the word budget? Then call it something different like, a spending plan, money plan, anything that makes you comfortable and puts your mind at ease but pushes you to do what has to be done to take you to the next level in living in prosperity abundantly.

A budget in its simplest form is your plan expressed in numerical terms. The Oxford dictionary defines a budget as "An estimate of income and expenditure for a set period of time."

A budget is about choices on how you plan to spend the income earned from employment and in business. You are empowered to make the choices on behalf of your family, business or place of employment This is a serious consideration on our stewardship not only on the resources that the Lord has placed in our hands, but also on the effects our decisions have on our family and businesses. As such, each choice needs to be carefully considered, as the impacts will have far reaching either negative or positive consequences. Decisions today will determine the resources you and others enjoy in the future.

A budget cannot and will never happen on its own; it takes time, commitment and dedication to get it done well. Now you gained an in-depth understanding of where you are, developed a basic financial plan, we can now start working on the budget. Each individual, family, business and organization's circumstances and situation is unique due to differences in vision, plan, goals, available resources and stated objectives. When preparing the budget it needs to match your purpose as currently defined by the Lord and the requirements of your business.

What is the purpose of your budget?

Chapter 8: Budgeting with purpose

A budget may serve many purposes such as planning, forecasting, communicating and motivating. The aim of this book is to help individuals and businesses create a budget that supports their purpose. I need you to return to the note pad where you recorded the purpose for doing a budget and review it. This purpose is the central driving force to decide how and where your income will be spent.

Time to return to the note pad, iPad, tablet, laptop, and let us start working together on your budget. In business, there are two main types of budgets; capital and operating. I will not go into much detail on creating budgets for businesses in this book; our focus will be on preparing a personal budget for you and your family.

The personal budget has two main elements; income and expenses. To refresh your memory on the meaning of income and expenses feel free to re-read the section on surplus or deficit. Whilst many did budgets before, the majority are not aligned to a plan or purpose. You already completed your self-assessment, financial plan, defined the purpose of the budget so you are ahead of the game.

The template will be used as the guide to complete the budget.

Personal Budget						
Month						
	Week 1	Week 2	Week 3	Week 4	Week 5	Total
Income						
Salary & Wages						
Commissions						
Bonuses						
Gratuity						
Overtime						
Pensions						
Total Income						
Mandatory Expenses						
Tithes (10%)						
Offerings						
Savings (10%)						
Seed Sowing						
Total Mandatory Expenses						
Fixed Expenses						
Rent/Mortgage						
Loan Payments						
Car Payments						
Insurance Premium						
Total Fixed Expenses						
Variable Expenses						
Electricity						
Telephone						
Groceries						
Fuel						
Entertainment						
Total Variable Expenses						
Surplus or Deficit						

The first column is to record your income. What is the purpose of your income? Is it to feed your family, support your lifestyle, sustain your business, help the needy, save for a rainy day? When you figure out the purpose of income, its places you in the best position to manage it effectively. Take the time to figure out the purpose of your income. The income that you have placed in the budget has a purpose each day remind yourself of that purpose.

The second section records the mandatory expenses. As a believer in Christ, the Bible teaches us that the first deduction that should be made from your income is to be given to the Lord. We are financial stewards responsible for managing the income God has given to us. He has given us life and health to earn the income, ensure that you honour him first.

The other sections are the fixed and variable expenses; each fulfils a specific purpose. Take the time to review each expense item. It needs to be examined carefully in the context of your personal and business plan. Are your expenses still relevant if not, take the time now to revise them now so that they remain relevant to your financial plan?

When the budget template is complete, it should be in surplus or balanced. What if your expenses are higher than your income? Then there are two options available either increase your income or reduce your expenses. Four quick suggestions to increase your income; work overtime, get a second or another job, use your talent and improve your marketability. Four ways to reduce your expenses; eliminate unnecessary spending, manage borrowing, controlling credit card usage and buy only what you need.

A budget is nothing new and has been around for many years. Why do budgets fail?

Chapter 9: Reasons Budgets Fail

"And let us not be weary in well doing: for in due season we shall reap, if we faint not."
Galatians 6:9 KJV

Through various forums, I will receive feedback from both individuals and businesses, saying I have tried this budgeting exercise and it does not work. Is this your position? Five common reasons budgets fail are; lack of discipline, lack of commitment, unrealistic expectations, negative attitude and lack of motivation.

Most individuals by nature are not disciplined. To achieve your vision, goals and objectives in business and personal life takes discipline. From the beginning of time, we did not want to obey God's rules and laws. In my opinion, this is the fundamental reason society is this way today. Discipline takes training and courage to change our behaviour. From today onwards we need to start to train ourselves, family, co-workers and others to become disciplined, this will allow us to achieve our purpose in life. A budget requires discipline to prepare and the most important part is that it takes even greater discipline to adhere to it – this is so critical for success.

I am committed! Sure, you heard this many times. Are you committed to ensuring the realisation of your business and life's vision? Do you intend for this to be a one-day exercise or do you plan to turn it into a lifetime commitment. Most of us are committed when things are working in our favour but the minute a challenge or obstacle comes our way, we are ready to quit.

The Bible in the book of Galatians, Chapter 6, verse 9 says "And let us not be weary in well doing: for in due season we shall reap, if we faint not." Never quit, even when it seems impossible, stick to the challenge and see it through to the end. To be successful in business and life it takes commitment this is not a one-day journey! Success is built upon doing the right thing every day, every moment, all the time – there are no excuses. . A budget requires your commitment otherwise; it becomes an exercise in futility.

How many individuals and businesses set goals and targets, which are not achievable? My grandmother taught me, "Never put your hat where you can't reach it". When you set goals for yourself or business, they need to realistic in the context of your current situation and resources available. They need to be SMART!

The same applies to the budget; it needs to realistic to match your situation, if not it will fail. For example, a married man with a wife and two children earning a monthly income of ten thousand dollars ($10,000) plans to save nine thousand ($9,000) every month. Such a goal given the need to pay the mortgage, purchase groceries and maintain the family for the month may not be the best thought out goal.

A positive approach brings positive results, a negative approach produce negative results. Is your purpose in life to be successful or fail? Should it be the latter then you do not need any assistance because by doing nothing it will happen on its own. Is your passion in life to be successful? The Bible teaches that Death and life are in the power of the tongue (Proverbs 18:21). Start speaking positively and look at the results in your business and personal life over the next six (6) months. What's does my approach have to do with my budget? It is central to the process; if you do not start with the right attitude then you are destined for failure from the start.

How motivated are you to do a budget right now? I am guessing not too motivated. Motivation is a key aspect in driving a person to succeed. It is the fuel, which enables you to move forward when challenges present themselves. What is your motivation to do a budget? Is it to become financially independent, to get out of debt, to retire in the best lifestyle? I want you to keep at the front of your mind that the vision motivating you must be consistent with purpose.

What are some of benefits of doing a budget?

Chapter 10: Benefits of Budgeting

From today onwards, think of your budget not as a nuisance but as a necessary tool to support you in achieving your financial goals.

There are many benefits to individuals, businesses, governments, non-profit organizations in doing a budget. The following seeks to highlights some of these benefits:

1. Financial stability and security;
2. A means of motivation;
3. Building a right example for your family;
4. To enable you to achieve your short, medium and long term goals;
5. A personal management tool for your finances;
6. Control over spending;
7. Forecasting;
8. Planning to efficiently use resources;
9. To control activities of the business.

Conclusion

The government will continue to put forward their budgets annually. The time has come for us to hold them accountable as the stewards over the country's finances. Are you going to continue to accept budget deficits moving forward? Information empowers you with the knowledge to make the right choices and decisions, take the time to understand how the national budget influences you, your business and community.

The time to prepare your budget is now, no need to delay any longer. You are accountable for managing your personal and business finances. The budget is a key tool and involves three simple steps; a self-assessment, a plan and the budget.

The self-assessment helps you to understand your current financial position. Your assets should be greater than your liabilities; it will improve your net worth. Your expenses should be less than your income; it positions you in a better place financially. If these are not so currently, put together a plan to get them in the right way.

The three key elements for your financial plan are; purpose, goals and timeframe or period. Purpose is critical to the plan, as it is the central driving force. The budget needs to match purpose to achieve success. Goals are essential to the plan and must be aligned with purpose and have relevant time lines.

You are born for a purpose. Each day remind yourself of that purpose, it would help you to keep focused until your plans are fully realized.

If this book has been a blessing to you feel free to recommend it to your friends, family, co-workers and other people that you come into contact. Please don't forget to leave a review of my book at your favourite retailer.

My prayer is that the Lord blesses you and may you submit your life to Him; and remember that as you plan and implement that plan supplement your life and your plan with prayer!

Examples of Assets

Artwork & Paintings
Bank Accounts - Savings, Checking
Buildings
Car/Motor Vehicle/Truck
Collectibles
Collectibles - Toys , Gadgets
Computers & Laptops
Credit Union Shares
Electronics
Equipment
Fixed Deposits
Furniture
Government Bonds
Home
Insurance Policies
Investment Accounts
iPad; Tablets
Jewellery
Mobile Phone
Mutual Funds - Unit Trust, Roytrin etc...
Pension Plan
Printer
Real Estate
Retirement Account/Fund
Stocks & Shares
Tools

Examples of Liabilities

Bank Loans
Bank Overdraft
Car Loans
Credit Cards
Credit Union Loans
Hire Purchase
Loans (Others)
Mortgage

About the Author

Junior C.A Pedro, FCCA is the founder and
Managing Director of JC Solutions Caribbean
Limited a company that provides value added
Consultancy, Accounting and Training services to
enable organizations improve their operational
efficiency and performance.

I am a qualified Chartered Accountant with over
fourteen years experience in various organizations
within the public and private sector of Trinidad and
Tobago. I am currently a member of the Association
of Certified Chartered Accountants (ACCA) and
hold a Post Graduate Diploma in Project
Management from Henley.

www.ingramcontent.com/pod-product-compliance
Lightning Source LLC
Chambersburg PA
CBHW070717180526
45167CB00004B/1510